Stone Venus

Jo Reed was born near Durham in 1941. She spent her childhood moving up and down the East Coast, from Northumbria to Norfolk, before arriving in Soho, London in the 1960s. She later lived in rural Surrey and Lincolnshire, before settling in Scarborough, North Yorkshire, at the turn of the century.

She has worked as an illustrator, printmaker and teacher, and recently completed an MA in Creative Writing from Newcastle University. Echoes of these pursuits and places appear throughout *Stone Venus*, which is her first collection of poetry.

Stone Venus

JO REED

for Val

Reed

VALLEY

STONE VENUS

First published in 2011
by Valley Press
www.valleypressuk.com

Printed in England by Imprint Digital,
Upton Pyne, Exeter

© 2011 Jo Reed
All rights reserved

The right of Jo Reed to be identified as author
of this work has been asserted in accordance with Section
77 of the Copyright, Designs and Patents Act 1988

This book is sold subject to the condition that it shall not,
by way of trade or otherwise, be lent, resold, hired out,
or otherwise circulated without the publisher's prior
consent in any form of binding or cover other than that
in which it is published and without a similar condition,
including this condition, being imposed on the
subsequent purchaser.

ISBN: 978-0-9568904-1-2
IPN: VP0013

A catalogue record for this book
is available from the British Library

www.valleypressuk.com/authors/joreed

9 8 7 6 5 4 3 2 1

CONTENTS

Embarkations 11
Wedding Weeds 12
Satyr 13
Piccadilly Circus 14
Life Class 15
Party Night at Freida's 16
Vanity 17
Woman Drinker 18
Afterthought 19
Interrogation 20
Move to Maesglas 21
A Suffolk Romance 22
Two Crows 23
Things Fall From The Sky 24
Underground 25
Waiting for the Waverley 26
Villendorf in Wedgwood 28
Passion Caged 29
Hurtwood Hill 30
Hill Farm 31
The Seamstress 33
Making Silk 34
Corvid 35
Passerine 36
Petunia Petulata 37
Minotaur 38
Keeping Watch 40
Side Ward 41

Clandestini 42
Recipe for a Disaster 43
Violin Section, 1941 44
Valentine, 1952 46
Memory of Venus 47
Exit Stage Left 48
Shaken Not Stirred 49
September, 1958 50
Treasure Chest, 2010 51
Yellow Bowl 52

Acknowledgements

Thanks go to Bill Herbert and Sean O'Brien, for the inspirational teaching of Creative Writing at Newcastle University; to Carte Blanche for their fellowship and encouragement; to Messrs. Maguire & Tickell with whom I enjoyed the journey; to Jackie Kay who 'gave permission'; to my sister Wendy for her steadfast belief in me, and my supportive family in Wales.

*for James and Jonathan,
my selkie sons*

Embarkations

I am a poet of embarkations.
I write in a flat with its back
to the Esplanade and quay,
facing the westerly winds
funneled in from the other sea.
There are many rooms,
that empty and fill with the tide.
Here an old life pours down
steep stairs, skips its way
right into the local landfill site.

There, another slides through gaps
in the rot of old sash windows,
insinuates itself between
bookshelves and lapsed memories,
flourishes in the spotted leaves
of a Begonia Rex. Another cutting.
A late propagation, written in,
taking root here by the margin,
readied for another journey.

Wedding Weeds

Was it the pink patterned jacket,
the hippy beads, that had her staring
so po-faced out of the photograph?
Secured in a black Barathea coat
she moved forward, best handbag
clutched chest high, a shield
against their laughter, taking point,
an armoured matron of honour.

Scents of cedar wood and camphor
drifted over sparse municipal tulips
in the green Public Library garden.
She scowled at the lens, at the Bride's
black strapped shoes, at the Best Bloke.
'This isn't a joke,' she hissed, tearful,
as they waited in the Registry office,
queuing for broken promises, lost dreams.

Satyr

There he is again
pointing his ears in my direction.
Hooves clattering along
the brass rail at the bar
of the French – his eyes akimbo
peering over the whisky,
whispering endearments
to all and sundry, especially
the visiting barmaid.

At table, his fingers click,
waiters are berated. Tales retold,
folded sweetly in a pocket
of the Jermyn Street jacket,
for later. Cloven feet tucked neat
under the shiny Terraza stool.

She listens, leaning sideways,
eyes and mouth forming O's
of interest,
as the satyr's eyes roam
beyond her, rake the room,
seeking the next enchantment.

Piccadilly Circus

The first time he caught a ball,
the pandemonium that whirled
inside his head fell into place.
Stuttered sound was stilled,
the silence became filled
with sounds of juggling fire.

The muscle and speed needed
to fly trapeze eluded him –
like the nerve and poise required
to soft shoe the city's high wires.
As clown, he could stagger, fall down,
be detained with the best of them.

In baggy trews and Oxfam shoes,
face painted bright with delight
at circling the ring with stars,
he tamed night's tigers: stalks
wild elephants beyond the castle,
fox-trots with Eros twice nightly.

Life Class

She drops her wrap over the back
of the blue painted chair, torn
Chinese folds shabbily exposed.

Moving to the dais she becomes Sphinx,
or Queen of Sheba, glances at the clock,
places a worn hand on the chalk mark.

She swivels her head to one side, stares –
a serpentine Cleopatra, embossed on time,
her breasts shivering until she settles.

Entering her daily trance, she hears again
the morning call, the scratch and scrape
of charcoal on cartridge, distant doors.

Silk markets of ancient Alexandria blend
with dusty floors, she begins to dream
of front page fame, portrait pored over.

She becomes other, descends comatose
to her barge on the darker Nile; enters
bleak palaces on the arms of Poet Princes,

takes lovers without number, loses her wits
in public places to great acclaim, still adored,
great Goddess of Debauchery, riven to her core.

Party Night at Freida's

Can you hear the candy skeleton
clicking at the bedpost
brushing the bright ribbons
braided into her black hair?

Her dark eyes blaze,
that impassive gaze
fixed on the cobalt jug
of day glowing marigolds
setting in the burnished glass.

Smoking through the sultry night,
swimming on waves of mariachi,
lot finally cast,
bones already thrown, her fate
interpreted by white clad nurses
whispering behind the throne.

Guardian lilies stand tall, heady
witness to night's addictions.
Her past parades the room in full panoply,
steals segments of fruit from the table,
spits pips and peel onto the street,
through the indigo door
left open for the dear departed.

Vanity

We watched you in the windows
of Joshua Taylor – dashing in lilac
on supercharged Saturdays.
Dancing at the Dorothy,
electrified by your own beauty,
you bared lupine teeth into the
smiling surfaces of silver teapots.

You admired your reflection
in the red and yellow decor,
the hard steel coffee machine
at the counter of the Kardomah;
in my green swimming eyes
by the river Cam, the hall mirror
at Willow Walk, where we tore
our stolen perch apart for tea.

Now, I see you on railway platforms
your perfect profile on the turn;
in the New York drawings (your own
constant model) the afternoon light
at four o'clock, leaving the cinema
as Humphrey Bogart or Belmondo,
Japanese wallpaper whenever I weep.

Woman Drinker

Red berried cherried
viscous campari, sharp
sweet iced sour within
a triangular goblet,
meniscus still steady.
A glass fan reflecting
the glare of all
who desired her,
held in front of
the bared red lips
that denied all
except liquid love.

Afterthought

If she had known she would sleep alone
in her borrowed marriage bed,
she'd have packed that life in a suitcase,
she'd have hitch-hiked to Brighton instead.

Interrogation

Surely there must be something to say in your defence, sir?
Did you not attempt to sweep away all trace of the black fear
whenever the old grey ghosts came tapping at the window?
Did you not put food on the table when there was little elsewhere,
keep the great wolf at bay through those dark and dangerous years?
Did you not look forward in hope through troubled times
to a more golden age of peace and tranquillity? You did?
Then sir, we must declare you fit to plead.

Move to Maesglas

A different view of death, this,
from the back bedroom window.
Ostentatious black surfaces
lettered in bright gold,
glitter shoulder high, celebrate
distinguished, Methodist death.

Then the recent monuments,
embroidered with silk flowers,
colour washed loss inside
opaque curtains of rain, wet
glass chippings, marbled stone.

Beyond the pale wall,
a small Celtic cross,
laced with moss and mould
the colour of my mother's eyes.

A Suffolk Romance

Labyrinths of lavender
take a covert path, where,
hidden in hollyhocks,
gently beached
against high flint cliffs,
Quince Cottage lies.

Timeworn timbers hold
the moon's tidal surges,
as green horizons
wash velvet over the village.

Her thatched sails set nightly,
tacking against magenta skies,
trawling lucent moth wings,
the scent of rosemary
in her warm wake.

Two Crows

Two crows claw
noisy passage
across open fields,
scream at the wind.

We watch them,
entwined in anger
over a red morsel
in the white world
of an early snowfall.

Things Fall From The Sky

Things fall from the sky –
marauding kites,
weathered balloons and
mutilated pheasants,
a frog dropped by a hungry heron.
Tickertape abandoned by
sub-prime creditors on
monopolied city streets,
aged propellers from older engines.
Meteorites, evidence of last night's
visitation from Mars.
Blessings and blasphemies
from cumulonimbus
attempting the anvil ending.
A cuckoo's guilty secrets.

Underground

Cases are trundled like unwilling dogs,
heavy with the stuff of empty dreams
along endless extremes of corridor
with steel barriers marked "no troll**s."

Circling around, lost, and aggressive
as blind moles shifting earth, they claw
their way to platform one westbound,
already full of exhausted commuters.

The tube arrives with a rush of stale air,
conflicting announcements of delays,
cancellations, 'an incident on the line.'
An anxious shouldering in crowded space,

as he takes the last place, doors hiss and clunk
giving respite. Eye contact is avoided.
No one speaks. The heavy silence expands
as they slowly detour death at Euston.

Waiting for the Waverley

She appears, detaches from the murk,
snouting heavily
around shifting secretive sandbars
at a leisurely pace.
Finally, grinding against a wooden jetty
facing north.

Heavy ropes snake around stanchions
as she's made fast,
binding her tight against the strain
of a turning tide.
Her great frayed cords creak, groan,
take up the refrain.

A clanging of bells
and sing-song orders. Passengers leave,
face the flatlands
of New Holland, the drab morning cold.
Engines sound,
readying the return against a tiderace,
hard labour
in choppy brown wastewater sliding to the sea.

We churn majestically
across to a city that's bursting its banks.
Another birthing,
poorly lit companionways,
confined spaces, the porthole views
of intensive care.

More waiting, then the vast estuary rises,
claims us again
for dusk's return voyage, an evening train,
disembarkation into nowhere.

Villendorf in Wedgwood

I sit and wait, my time is near.
It's always near. All I have to do

is recline in my ancient place, stay
very still in another's captive will.

I anticipate windsong, and tideturn,
soft seed-set in a thin sickled moon.

Creating a small space in this one
for months beyond number, I fired

her fickle nightlongings, and now
the marks are there, burnished in.

His charcoal eyes burn into mine,
I feel his palm smooth my earthen thigh.

And yes, his slender body will heave
within my clay, through the porcelain

of this pretty shell, where my riverine
being hardens under her lustred glaze.

She is just an empty mermaid's purse
waiting to nurture all that will be mine.

Passion Caged

It smoulders in secret
corners and crevices,
being exceptionally
sensitive to touch.

Mainly nocturnal, it
can usually be revived
in daylight hours
by the scent of violets,
a sidelong glance, or
a glass of Bardolino.

Please stay this side of the bars,
just in case it infiltrates
a reflective moment,
that empty space.

Do not feed with
sweetness and love,
a surfeit could be
fatal.

Hurtwood Hill

We fled the clutch of diseased elms,
our midnight keep, and snaked away
through water blackened lanes,
never reaching the twin beams ahead.

Once, on the slick tarmac'd surface,
slight creatures slithered through
our rain splintered sights, trapped
between your stony glance,
my windscreen's obscured view.

In the arc light's empty spool, shapes
sidled out of range, feathered the edge
of our dark visions, too fast to track
their spoor into the Deepdene forest.

Switchbacks shunted us down the lane,
into addertime. Marks and symbols
detonated our inkling histories,
short circuited, setting truth aflame.

We reversed, drove back the way we came.

Hill Farm

1. Winter

Lilac sheep pull at the last
yellow shoots of the day,
tracing their way down
long fingers of shadow.
Huge skies, swollen with
the last of autumn's rain
fall hard into the fields.
Trees lean precariously
against the late arriving
cold front, shivering
in anticipation. I walk
up toward window lights,
a bowl of parsnip soup.
Safe inside, I lean against
the warm stove, inhale
winter's woodsmoke.

2. Spring

Mizzling mist makes
its way up the valley
ahead of bitter rain.
Bones of dead sheep
intone DNA dialects
at the blinded stones
that once ordered and
bordered their lives.
Sturdy ghosts of farmers
from Llanybither, click
shrivelled tongues at
burning pyres, that defy
all ancient boundaries.
Exhausted, she sits,
waiting for the crack
of his percussion gun.

The Seamstress

Gifts of eggs, lemon and virgin oil,
fill the sewing table with their plenty.
The cat, frozen furred from the night,
scratches for attention at the sill
as seasoned olive wood still sings,
glowing like summer in whitened ash.
She sets aside her coffee, yawning,
opens the heavy door to the day,
sees olive and walnut trees, the snows
of Albania, white in the morning light.
She listens for the long distance call
that will answer all the questions.
The cat shakes snow from his paws
settles, purring, on her knee to wait.

Making Silk

Only when stripped of their young are moths freed to fly;
unencumbered by the weight of their past,
they drift up to the moon,
wings disintegrating in the cold light.

Corvid

After that day, when a cold
empty grief came into being,
her small sounds of protest
became indiscreet cackles
at inappropriate moments.

The Custodian, unnerved
by strange scuttlings, fervent
seeking of words in back-alleys
and threadbare hall carpets,
silverstreamed to sunshine states.

Fine threads of black down
emanated from follicles
in translucent cream skin,
as her chapped legs developed
rhymes of yellowing scales.

She hid opinions in silken gauze,
layers of purple pashmina.
Inside her new winter boots,
painted claws shone siren red.

She couldn't wait to clap her wings.

Passerine

Bedraggled, featherworn,
she perches on the edge of a word,
surrounded by detritus,

discarded puzzles of paper, crumpled
receipts and small deceits,
transportable objects,
lustre lost, ready to pawn.

Blunted beak quests, picks, ponders,
jettisons just enough
to leave a space to dream.

Scraps fall softly
between scissors and stone,
flower into song.

Petunia Petulata

You'll find me
standing at the foot of the stairs,
suitcase packed
ready to roll spiteful wheels
in parallel lines
across perfectly raked gravel,
bruising
your award winning
petunias, just before
I snap
the gate
shut.

Minotaur

Sometimes,
I hide in shadowed corners
trying to breathe,
my chest heaves with
the dust of digging.

Sometimes,
they hang bread at the gate
with pitchers of Mavrodaphne
that dulls the pain,
magnifies my angers.

Sometimes,
the sound of my coughing
runs around the tunnels,
frightens me as it funnels
its violent echoes.

Sometimes,
they send fair companions
who ignore my rough speech,
can't groom my knotted hair,
or love me, once they see.

Sometimes,
Screaming, they try to kill me,
I fight back,
filling the air with the song
of my black bladed axe.

Sometimes,
I eat their flesh, to satisfy
my hunger for humanity,
as I hack my way
toward the sound of the sea.

Keeping Watch

Look steadily for
a long time through
cubes of sugared glass,
hold your breath
with determination,
conceal your identity.

Wait at the outskirts
of a powdered city
wound in bindweed,
inhabited by retired subalterns
and pallid poppy drinkers.

Aeronautical scientists
weigh anchors with feathers,
chart progress
under a cloak of anaesthesia.
Watch, as children, recently
appointed ghosts, drift through
the lost lives of volunteers
as violent memories.

Wear white gloves
so as not to make a mark,
unless it is to erase
black lines from paper.

Side Ward

A moist ventricle, harassed at the portal,
pauses momentarily to reflect. Her pulse,
slippery and sly tonight, fights, subverts
the digital clicking at the column top.

A scent of calm catastrophe pervades,
invades that narrow space behind sleep
and sight, between the serpent's call,
tomorrows dark and uninvited dawn.

Waspish young day staff disinfect,
soothing dust into corners, garrulous
in their need to escape bleached silence,
the tell-tale tick of heart monitors.

Clandestini

So, my just reward,
this slice of Italian earth.
After all my labours.
I sleep soundly here.

I cared for your father
as you worked in the city,
prepared salads daily
in factories lines;
made garments in back streets,
and held your child nightly,
until she fell asleep to
Brazilian lullabies.
I washed you mother's hair
when she was beyond caring.
I polished hospital corridors
and swept your town squares,
while you were at prayer,
in the blind heat of summer.

Now in this ground
with my marker in place,
you acknowledge my being,
have allotted me a space.

Recipe for a Disaster

First strip away my dignity.
Separate me from all I know,

as I migrate from hate and fear
during smoke darkened years.

Incriminate my children
as soon as they are born.

Debate oil and water rights
in air conditioned lobbies

while I dehydrate at night
beside the village graves.

Re-allocate my bag of grain
to lighten your burial burden.

Wait for deserts to displace
my bones, as I drown in sand.

Violin Section, 1941

Musical slaves, we mark time,
accompany automatons morning march
into frozen fields beyond the wire,
beguile them back with Brahms each night.

Dreaming myself into that canvas village, I hear
Chagall's be-hatted fiddler, serenely centred,
singing blue and green contentment.

Does he know about us?

Our ceremonies are conducted
in icy railway sidings,
grey passages between life and hope.
Our eyes slide down the scales.
We cannot meet their gaze,
yet witness the last rites,
divergences:
the quick – left, to enslavement,
the dead walk right – toward the fire.

Maestros pour broken notes
into misappropriated scores:
weakened waltzes, mild mazurkas,
easing torn peoples past uniform hate,
toward the unimaginable, with the familiar.

Our lives depend on every note.

Bowing and scraping at guilt and lies
we perform.
Tears freeze our breath,
music perverted
into an instrument of death.

Valentine, 1952

They had rested at the edge of the lake,
where stilled mountain waters reflected
a dead Maharajah's grandiose dreams.

Closely observed by dragonflies
and white egret, their sunburnt bodies
refracted light in its silted olive depths.

Beside the stack of folded khaki clothes,
a despatch box waited, at attention,
their embarkation orders still unopened.

He drains the bottle, one golden shot for each man lost,
his first line of defence against the overwhelming odds
of the staffroom; the desk, the cloying comfort of women.

Looking down through filigree bars
at Warwick square below, he listens
to the city's late night murmurings.

Slitting open the heavy pink envelope
with a ceremonial kukri, he releases
the scent of sandalwood. Just enough

to pierce his heart. Green sediments
flood his vision, drown Miss Johnson's
rounded, carefully camouflaged hand.

Memory of Venus

Another cold day beachcombing,
predatory gaze directed down
at exposed shingle, bamboo roots,
and old cuttlefish bones,
shifted by the cuspid sands.

It was a real find, a flint,
scoured smooth by attrition.
Venus de Milo in miniature,
decapitated by wind, waves,
and ancient alpine ice flows.

This curvaceous white form,
thinner than any Celtic queen,
glowed hard-square, from
within her dessicated throne
of blackened bladderwrack.

Only the core of her left –
a memory of being whole.
I keep her upon my bookshelf,
hold her neat within my hand,
reminded of the life in stone.

Exit Stage Left

Just for the sake of recovering
your dignity my good sir, did you
have to put paid to that character
in the last scene? There she was,
almost tart perfect, velvet stomacher
a slightly tight fit. She had acted
her part in bits of old brocade for
many a sad moon sir – Mistress, Hussif,
Pregnant Pause, Grieving Mother,
Lost Soul – and now? Perhaps play
Wardrobe Mistress? She can still sew
and mend a wounded heart. Without
strong seams and stitches, old tapestries,
like your performance sir, just fall apart.

Shaken Not Stirred

Crammed into a lift, I'm fending off
fledgling Flemings, uncomfortably encased
in their hired suits.
Mob-handed, they descend, testosterone
overlaid with Aramis from faraway Fenwicks.

Glossed girls teeter on vertiginous Versace,
satin flags fly against dreaming thighs,
imperfections smoothed with silken dusts
'for one night only'
they reel and shimmer in cinematic style.

Surrounded by miniature Ken men –
modelled on base older templates –
I sigh, marvel at the brave Barbarellas,
these assassins-to-be,
more unsung heroes. Just glad it's not me.

September, 1958

I remember that first school dance,
the hand hemmed A-line skirt,
flat black shoes, and white ankle socks.
I remember envying all the girls
swanning around in lisle stockings,
as I was taught to tango, and waltz,
by a conscripted 6th year flirt.
I remember the hollow delights
of Heartbreak Hotel, Miss Molly's
wild ways on Saturday nights,
as we jived round corners, shocking
them at the palais, with imitations of
Chuck Berry's not-so-sweet sixteens,
paler versions of the American dream.
Now, in artists smock and denim jeans,
black oversize specs, another me.
I remember, and pull-on the new
blue suede shoes, a generous size three.

Treasure Chest, 2010

I hear the sound of the simple catch,
the click that kept my treasures safe.
My christening bracelet, VE day ribbons
a delicate glass ornament.

In the fifties, inside my locker, it held
a traveller's sewing kit; a metal thimble,
curved darning needle, always threaded
with grey wool, elastic, and 4711 cologne.

Later, at Warkworth Terrace,
in the top drawer of a bed-sit tallboy,
it protected woodblock tools, paper money,
extra nibs for a lost mapping pen.

Yesterday, I unpacked the small munitions box,
softened with fabric from another world,
where people were not at war.
The crackled letters still spell out my name.

Yellow Bowl

On the table by the stair
a gold plastic angel's wing
flies along the bright rim
of a cinnamon yellow bowl.

On the windowsill,
a painted lady lies still
in the cold summer morning,
eyes wide open.